UNIVERSITY OF OX

ASHMOLEAN MUSE

ARCHAEOLOGY, ARTEFACTS
AND THE BIBLE

by

P. R. S. MOOREY

OXFORD

Printed for the Visitors and
sold at the Ashmolean Museum

1969

Printed in Great Britain by Alden & Mowbray Ltd.
at the Alden Press, Oxford

Notes

1. The numbers which appear in the list of illustrations are the serial numbers of the objects in the accessions registers of the Department of Antiquities.
2. Measurements are expressed in metres and parts of a metre.
3. The following abbreviations are used in the references to dimensions: H Height; L Length; W Width; D Diameter.
4. Full details of the objects illustrated will be found in the 'List of Illustrations'; the captions are considerably abbreviated in many cases.
5. A diagrammatic chronological chart covering Egypt, Palestine and Mesopotamia will be found at the end of this booklet.

Acknowledgements

I am most grateful to Mr. R. W. Hamilton, Keeper of the Ashmolean Museum, for his advice and assistance in preparing this essay, to Miss O. M. Godwin and Mrs. D. Carpenter for the photography and to Mrs. Pat Clarke for drawing the diagram and maps.

Contents

List of Illustrations

8   Three juglets of 'Tell el-Yahudiyeh' ware from the name site
    in the Egyptian delta.   H .110; H .093; H .097
                                    (1888.268; 1896–1908. E.3501, 3496)

9   The 'Weld-Blundell' prism inscribed with dynastic lists of
    the Kings of Sumer and Akkad from the antediluvian period
    to the end of the reign of Sin-magir, *c.* 1817 B.C., from Larsa
    in Iraq.   H .200   (1923.444)

10 A fragmentary tablet inscribed with part of the Babylonian
    Creation Epic from Mound 'W' at Kish in Iraq.   .140 × .056
                                                    (1926.373)

11 Late Bronze Age gold earrings and pendants from Tell el
    'Ajjul. 1949.305 (.080 × .040), 306 (.078 × .017), 307 (W .032),
    308 (W .037), 309 (W .055), 322 (D .010), 320 (D .013)

12 (*a*)   Glass 'Astarte' figurine from Tell ed-Duweir, *c.* 1400–
            1350 B.C.   H .055   (1955.501)

    (*b*)   Baked clay 'Astarte' plaque from Gezer, *c.* 1300–1200
            B.C.   .120 × .049   (1912.622)

    (*c*)   Faience affix in the shape of a female face from Gezer,
            c. 1300 B.C.   .070 × .059   (1912.620)

    (*d*)   Bronze statuette of a male deity from Sidon, *c.* 1400–
            1200 B.C.   H .088   (1886.1996)

13 Fragmentary tablet inscribed with a letter from the ruler of
    Byblos to the Pharaoh of Egypt from Tell el Amarna in
    Egypt, fourteenth century B.C.   .113 × .065 (1893.1–41: 408)

14 Baked clay bowl (restored) from Tell ed-Duweir inscribed in
    the Egyptian hieratic script with a record of wheat production
    for harvest taxes (?), *c.* 1230 B.C.   D .190   (1964.483)

15 Baked clay anthropoid coffin lid from Tell el-Yahudiyeh in
    the Egyptian delta, *c.* 1220–1150 B.C.   H .340   (1888.297)

16 Baked clay 'stirrup-jar' (restored) in the Philistine style from
    Tell el Far'ah (South), early twelfth century B.C.   H .125
                                                    (1930.558)

17 (*a*)   Ivory plaque decorated in the Egyptian manner with
            two men, wearing Egyptian royal crowns, flanking a
            'sacred tree'; from Fort Shalmaneser, Nimrud; eighth
            to seventh century B.C.   .096 × .056   (1962.601)

(*b*) Fragment of an ivory pyxis carved with a woman playing a Syrian lyre; from Fort Shalmaneser, Nimrud; eighth to seventh century B.C. .060 × .024 (1959.210)

(*c*) Illegible royal name in a feathered cartouche guarded by sphinxes in the Phoenician style, part of an ivory inlay; from Fort Shalmaneser, Nimrud, eighth to seventh century B.C. .090 × .040 (1960.1215)

18 Iron Age II pottery (*c.* 800 B.C.) from Jerusalem; all, save the little black juglet, were found in a cave associated with an extra-mural shrine. (bowls) 1964.492 (D .174), 493 (D. 227); (jugs, l. to r.) 1964.510 (H .121); 1967.853 (H .090); 1964-513 (H .121)

19 Inscribed stone altar from Palmyra, dated September A.D. 85, with an incense-altar (*hamman*) shown on the front. H .481 (C.2–9)

20 Modern impressions from two inscribed seals: (*a*) Smoky quartz seal of one Hosea, eighth to seventh century B.C. .019 × .015 (1921.1221)

(*b*) Red jasper seal of Mikneiah, son of Yehomelek, eighth to seventh century B.C. .014 × .012 (1943.2)

21 An ivory inlay fragment from Nimrud, Iraq, showing the fitter's marks on the back (on the front a stag grazing among lotus flowers; its head is lost); eighth to seventh century B.C. H .054; L .092 (1952.79)

22 Baked clay jar handle from Jerusalem stamped with an inscribed seal mentioning the city of Socoh, *c.* 700 B.C. H .116 (1968.1394)

23 Silver ear-rings and pendants of the Achaemenid period found in a coin hoard buried in Syria or Jordan by *c.* 450 B.C. 1967.761 (.024 × .013); 759 (H .020); 760 (.015 × .012); 771 (H .027); 764 (.029 × .012); 770 (D .017); 766 (.039 × .016); 767 (030. × .026); 768 (.020 × .041)

24 Fragment from the side of an Attic red-figure lekythos (small jug) from Tell el Far'ah (South) painted by the 'Beth-Pelet' painter, *c.* 450 B.C. H .085 (1930.550)

25 A series of Palestinian lamps: from left to right: 1954.591— Tomb G.37, Jericho, Middle Bronze

Age. L .133; 1956.1082—Tomb M.16,
Jericho. Early to Middle Bronze Age.
·040 × .105 1954.658:—Jericho, Roman,
first century A.D.   L .090; 1968.1436—
Jerusalem, first century B.C. .036 × .043
1954.659e—Jericho, Roman, first century A.D.   L .080

26   Handle from a baked clay Rhodian wine-jar, stamped
'Damokles'; from Jerusalem, *c.* 220–180 B.C.   W .160
(1958.67)

27   Group of Nabataean pottery from Petra, including a typical
painted Nabataean bowl. Left to right: 1963.1413 (H. 175);
1436 (H .086); 1439 (D .183); 1419 (L .073); 1421
(D .063)

28   Group of Roman pottery and glass vessels of the first century
A.D. from Jericho. Left to right: 646 (H .170), 644 (H .087),
649 (H .201); 1956.508 (H .123); 1954.659 (L .080); 1955.
515 (H .150), 513 (H.100)

29   Jar of the type used to store the 'Dead Sea Scrolls', first
century A.D.   H .626   (1951.477a, b)

Prologue

Nowhere is it more apparent than in museum displays that archaeology is the study of durable rubbish; even the intrinsically beautiful is ravaged by long deposit in the earth. The visitor seeing for the first time a display of Palestinian archaeology might be forgiven for yielding to an irresistible urge to move on to more pleasing or familiar things. The following essay is offered, not as an apology for archaeology—we hope the visitor will come to believe that it needs none—but as an invitation to look again and consider these battered objects in their wider context. No museum display, however artfully arranged or skilfully labelled, can evoke for the spectator the people and the period in which these objects were made, used and often treasured. This requires more knowledge than such a medium can alone provide fused with an imaginative sympathy which is the spectator's prerogative.

This booklet is intentionally brief, without, it is hoped, being cryptic. It should be possible to read it during a visit to the gallery with the objects immediately to view. A detachable sheet lists the exact location of each object illustrated in the text and a short bibliography includes a wide range of easily available books in English which explore in greater depth and detail many of the problems cursorily surveyed in this essay. The use of the word *essay* is deliberate. It is no more than an attempt to say in a few thousand words what Palestinian archaeology is about. But Palestinian archaeology is constantly changing its shape, as what may seem the case today is often shown, by tomorrow's finds, to have been a false conclusion based on inadequate evidence. If the reader is stimulated to correct and modify the perspectives of this essay from his or her own reading and looking, then much of its purpose will have been served.

ARCHAEOLOGY AND BIBLICAL STUDIES

Alone among the literature of the great religions of the world, the Bible is based upon the history of a people who believed that God's attitude to mankind, particularly His purpose for them as His chosen people, was revealed in historical events. There are indeed large portions of it devoted to spiritual, ethical and ritual instruction, as in all great religious books, but this is at all times subordinate to a profound belief that God has made and will continue to make himself known through human affairs.

It is this unique historical setting which makes archaeology such a vital part of biblical studies, for every biblical student is inevitably a student of ancient history in the widest sense. In very rare cases he will have contemporary written records at his disposal, more commonly he will be entirely dependent upon the evidence of objects used or made by man in antiquity: the subject-matter of archaeology. Yet it must always be remembered that archaeology is the handmaid of history not of theology. It cannot, indeed has never sought to, authenticate every aspect of the biblical narrative. It can only hope to throw light, of varying intensity, on the historical circumstances surrounding each event. In every case this has enhanced rather than diminished the Bible's interest and significance for readers so far removed in time and place from the events described there.

When reading the text of the Old Testament in the light of archaeological discoveries it has always to be borne in mind that it is not the work of a single author, written in a brief space of time. It is a whole library of books, each with a different and often very complex history of composition. The Old Testament as we have it today is the result of constant collecting, editing and arranging of very heterogeneous oral and written sources. The actual writing was extended over at least a thousand years from c. 1200 B.C.—the Song of Deborah, Judges v—to the second century B.C.—Esther. We have only to consider how English literature was modified in language, style and form between 'Beowulf' and 'Tristram Shandy' to realize the enormous changes in religious and intellectual ideas which this necessarily involves. Moreover, the Old Testament authors naturally varied greatly in

13

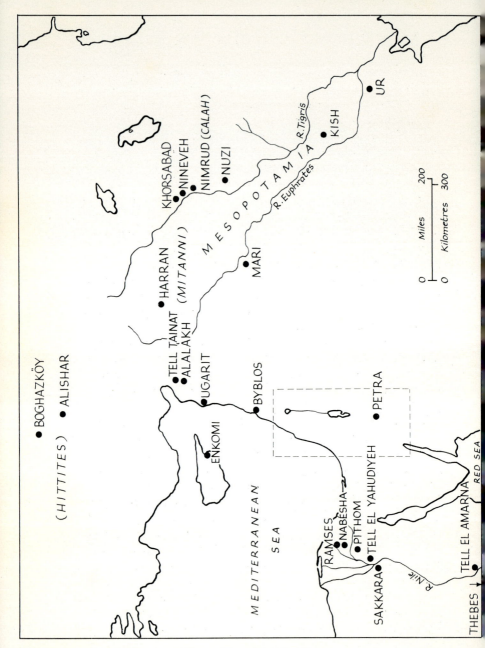

Fig. 1   Map of the Near East

competence and intention, some incorporating their ancient sources verbatim, others censoring and paraphrasing them. This could lead to two accounts of a single event (the Creation), over-simplified narratives of highly complex situations (the Conquest) and recurrent anachronisms introduced by later editors. Although the light archaeology has thrown on the historical growth of the Old Testament lies outside the range of this essay, its relevance to the question will constantly be apparent. It has revealed remarkable literary parallels in other ancient Near Eastern languages, it has provided evidence for the history of the Hebrew language and script and it has uncovered ancient biblical manuscripts which have greatly elucidated the study of the Hebrew Old Testament.

From the Middle Ages travellers in Palestine had become increasingly interested in the relation between the countryside around them, where considerable vestiges of ancient occupation had survived above ground, and the detailed accounts of the land familiar to them from the Bible. But apart from a few outstanding exceptions, notably the travels of Pietro della Valle published in Rome in 1650, and Adrian Reland's *Palaestina ex monumentis veteribus illustrata* of 1709, these men merely recounted journeys along well-known routes illustrated by anecdotes and observations of unequal interest. It was not until the nineteenth century that critical scientific study superseded ill-disciplined, if informed, curiosity.

The nature of this change is very well represented by its first great exponent, the American scholar Edward Robinson. In 1841 he published his *Biblical Researches in Palestine, Mount Sinai and Arabia Petraea in 1838*, which, by careful correlation of linguistic, historical and geographical evidence, transformed existing know-ledge of biblical topography and laid a secure foundation for all future work. With the establishment of the Palestine Exploration Fund in 1865 the way was open not only for the first controlled excavations, by Capt. Charles Warren at Jerusalem (1867–70), but for the detailed mapping of Western Palestine, a vital preliminary to any sound archaeological fieldwork, by Capts. Conder and Kitchener (1872–8).

The earliest excavators were long hampered by the absence of any system for dating objects not associated with historical inscriptions. In 1890 Flinders Petrie, after some years of exca-

15

vating in Egypt, demonstrated by cutting a vertical section through the ancient settlement mound at Tell el-Hesy, that each main period of occupation had distinctive types of pottery. By correlating this relative sequence with seals and rare inscriptions he worked out an absolute chronology. His scheme has been constantly modified, but never fundamentally altered.

For the next thirty years an international band of scholars excavated on sites of major importance: the British at Gezer and Jerusalem, the Germans at Ta'anach, Megiddo and Jericho and the Americans at Samaria, where Reisner considerably advanced the excavation techniques of the time. With the renewal of fieldwork in 1918 the number of expeditions increased significantly and, with an interval in the nineteen-forties, has never ceased to grow. The main developments alone can be noted here. Growing experience gradually stimulated greater attention to the analysis of stratigraphy, notably by Miss Kenyon at Jericho and Jerusalem (1952–67), and the correspondingly important pottery chronology, greatly advanced by Albright in excavations at Tell Beit Mirsim (1926–32). A new area of research was opened up in the field of prehistory, following excavations by Turville-Petre (1925) and Miss Garrod (1928–34) in Palestinian caves, which has developed rapidly in recent years through a happy alliance of archaeologists and natural scientists studying all evidence available from the region for the earliest history of human settlement. This is but one aspect of a realization that archaeological research must be directed, through careful survey work followed by selective excavation, to the solution of specific problems. In the field of biblical studies this has applied especially to a growing understanding of the complex archaeology of the Exodus and Conquest.

THE GEOGRAPHICAL SETTING AND ITS RELEVANCE

The term PALESTINE is used here to define the region from the river Litani in the north to the Negev in the south ('From Dan to Beersheba') and from the Mediterranean Sea in the west to the Arabian desert in the east. Hardly exceeding Wales in size it is nonetheless a region with considerable variations in climate and

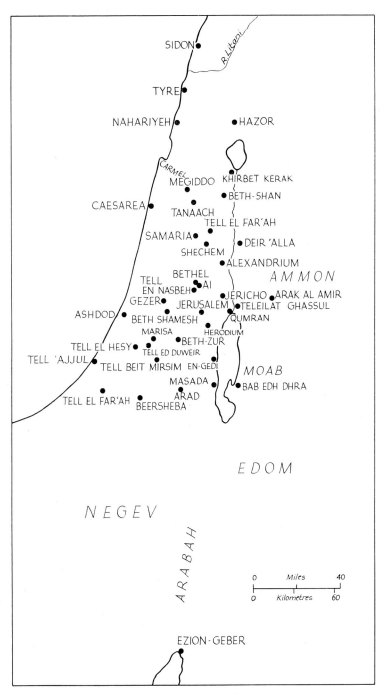

Fig. 2 Map of Palestine

landscape. The winters are generally wet and can be quite cold, the summers dry and hot. Climate naturally varies with the configuration of the land, with rainfall tending to decrease from west to east.

There are five main natural divisions, running from north to south:

I   *The Coastal Strip* (plains of Dor, Sharon and Philistia)

This is a narrow band of land with natural harbours north of the Carmel promontory, but none to the south. The plain of Philistia, heavily populated in antiquity, is particularly fertile.

II   *The Western Hills*

These limestone hills, with intervening plains and valleys, form both the geographical and historical backbone of the country, for here lay Galilee, Samaria and Judah. The fertile plains of Megiddo and Jezreel offer an important break, providing a low and easy route through from the coastal plain to Transjordan. Olive, fig and other fruit trees, as well as wheat and vines, flourish in Galilee; the hills of Judah are more barren, but those of the Shephelah, linked by valleys to the coastal plain, support vines, trees and grain crops. South of Beersheba the barren steppe region of the Negev, with slowly encroaching desert, has often in the past supported a sedentary population through careful control and regulation of available water supplies.

III   *The Jordan Valley*

This rift valley drops rapidly from 695 ft. below Sea Level at the Sea of Galilee to 1285 ft. below at the Dead Sea. The narrow flood plain supports dense thickets of shrub and tamarisk. Natural springs, as at Jericho, support occasional oases.

IV   *The Eastern Hills (Transjordan)*

Four major rivers cut through this high tableland, whose height ensures considerable rainfall and fertility, though this decreases eastwards and steppe rapidly gives place to desert. Bashan in the north was anciently renowned for its grain and cattle; Gilead in the centre produced grain, vines, olive, oak and pine; but as the fertile strip grows narrow in Moab so the agricultural productivity declines.

V *The Desert*

To the East and South-East of Palestine the great expanse of the Arabian desert stretches away into Syria, Iraq and Saudi Arabia.

The structure of Palestine had an important bearing on its historical development. It lies right across the narrow passage between sea and desert, barely a hundred miles wide, through which passed all communications between Africa and Asia. Through its harbours, maritime plains and inland valleys all traffic had to pass in peace and war. Set between sea and desert, the configuration of two mountain ranges, the absence of long rivers or broad alluvial plains and the uneven distribution of soil and rainfall, unlike the rich alluvial plains of Egypt and Mesopotamia, discouraged the formation of large unified, stable and wealthy societies. With rare exceptions the peoples of Palestine, whilst sometimes excelling their neighbours in religious and literary sensibility were poor, divided and at best precariously independent. The cultivated lands of Palestine and Syria held a perpetual attraction for the nomadic tribes of Arabia. Constant permeation of the population by settlers of Semitic speech and nomadic stock was consequently a dominant theme in the region's history.

In archaeology these factors are reflected in the relative poverty of material cultures; the recurrent intrusion or assimilation of Egyptian, Mesopotamian, Aegean and other foreign elements; and the periodic recessions and renewals of city life which are seen to indicate successive waves of penetration and settlement by Amorite, Canaanite, Aramaean, Hebrew or Arab tribesmen.

TELLS AND TERMINOLOGY

The sequence of events and cultures in Palestine, before the extensive use of writing, is inferred entirely from the superimposed strata of debris in ancient settlements. Valuable supplementary information is recovered from cemeteries and isolated graves. Houses of mud, mud-brick or rubble, with plastered walls and roofs, when they collapse leave little or nothing to salvage and a newcomer will merely level off the ruins and build above them. In the course of time accumulating debris formed a mound (*tell*) in which the sequence of remains can be observed and recorded by cutting trenches into it. Stratigraphy—observing the changes in a mound's growth—enables changes in architecture, techniques (pottery, metallurgy, etc.) and domestic equipment to be placed in order of time and related to observed interruptions or changes of settlement. In recent years the measurements of residual radioactivity in carbon specimens (Carbon 14) has added a source of absolute chronology for periods too early for synchronization with the historical chronologies of Egypt and Mesopotamia based on ancient king-lists from *c*. 3000 B.C.*

No system of chronological terminology has yet been invented which can register unambiguously the complex and differential growth of regional cultures in the Near East. In Palestine and Syria the current terms signify technological stages (*Neolithic, Chalcolithic, Bronze* and *Iron*) conventionally subdivided into three (Early, Middle and Late; and again I, II, III, etc.). The archaeological cultures typical of a particular phase in prehistory sometimes bear the name of the site on which it was first recognized: *Natufian, Tahunian, Ghassulian*. The matter is further complicated by the varying tempo of cultural development: plains and valleys tended to be more advanced than the hill country, whilst primitive ways of life long persisted on the desert periphery.

* Wherever appropriate the absolute dates in this essay, and in the Museum's display, are based on the so-called 'Middle Chronology' which is that generally adopted in the revised Cambridge Ancient History. (The reign of Hammurabi is thus dated from 1792 to 1750 B.C.; the First Dynasty of Babylon from 1894 to 1595 B.C.)

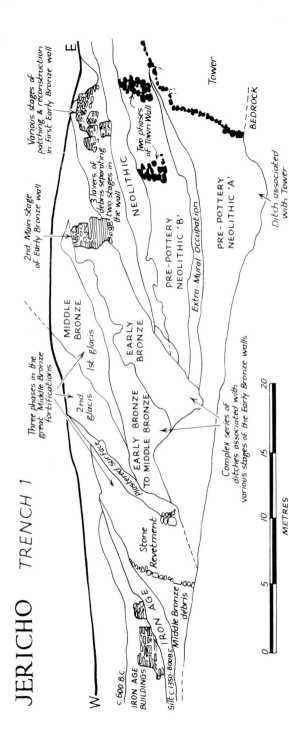

Fig. 3   Diagrammatic drawing of the Main Section through the *tell* at Jericho

PALESTINE BEFORE THE CANAANITES

Small nomadic bands, sometimes living in caves, sometimes camping in the open, depending on hunting, fishing, fowling and gathering wild fruits (MESOLITHIC), had probably been living in the Near East for a very long time before the earliest domestication of animals and cultivation of cereals, about twelve thousand years ago, led to a transformation in their way of life.

Most aspects of this change are now well known in Palestine. From *c.* 10,000 B.C. the *Natufians* occupied caves and rock-shelters where they were available, as in the Carmel region, or settled in the open, notably at Eynan and Jericho. Flint arrowheads, lavish use of animal teeth as ornaments and large numbers of wild animals' bones—gazelle, boar, hyena, leopard and bear—emphasize the importance of hunting. Although the presence of storage pits and flint sickle blades mounted in elaborately carved bone handles may only mean that the inhabitants reaped wild grains, they indicate a growing dependence on cereals. Stone pestles and mortars suggest that plant food was pulverized rather than rubbed down on querns. A monumental tomb at Eynan may be that of a tribal chief.

Although settled life, with domesticated animals and cultivated crops, has long been recognized as characteristic of the NEOLITHIC, it was only recently revealed that this was well advanced in Palestine before the introduction of pottery. This has led, it may be hoped temporarily, to the unwieldy term *Pre-pottery Neolithic*. This period is best represented in a village settlement at Beidha and at Jericho, where a remarkable series of stone built fortifications and elaborate provision for water or grain storage suggest that many features associated with urban life—social, economic and political organization—were also present before the use of pottery.

At Jericho this period has been divided into two phases. In the earlier ('A') when the fortifications were at their most impressive, the inhabitants still had close links with the hunters and food gatherers of the surrounding hills. Houses were small and circular, built of hog-backed bricks, with clay floors, some still retaining impressions of rush matting. Their successors ('B' or *Tahunian*)

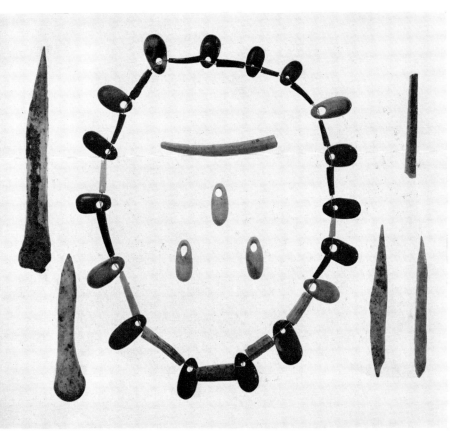

Plate 1   Mesolithic shell and bone necklace, and bone tools

were an entirely different people, who arrived, perhaps from Syria, with a fully developed urban way of life, to settle some time after the previous walled settlement had been abandoned. They had more elaborate rectangular houses with large rooms, built of cigar-shaped bricks with finger impressions to key the mortar. Floors and parts of walls were plastered, often painted cream and red, and burnished. There is the first conclusive evidence for domesticated animals, primarily goats, at this period. The preservation and plastering of human skulls, baked clay sculpture and a possible shrine reflect their religious practices. Turquoise

23

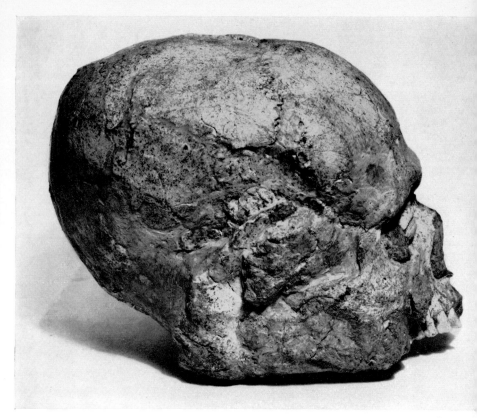

Plate 2   Pre-pottery Neolithic 'B' plastered skull from Jericho (Profile)

matrix, cowrie shells and obsidian indicate commercial relations with Sinai, the Mediterranean coast and Anatolia.

Pottery was introduced into Palestine by different groups penetrating into the country from different directions some time in the sixth millennium B.C. (*Pottery Neolithic*). Some older settlements were completely abandoned and new ones were established in increasing numbers all over the country. Throughout the period there was an absence of substantial building; huts and pit-dwellings sufficed. The newcomers were farmers who settled in small communities wherever there was water and cultivable soil, breeding cattle, sheep and pigs in addition to the

24

Plate 2   Pre-pottery Neolithic 'B' plastered skull from Jericho (Face)

already domesticated goat. The fine stonework of the earlier period gives way to crudely worked stone bowls and there were changes in the flint techniques. At the moment this period, which may well have lasted over a thousand years, is one of the most obscure in Palestinian prehistory.

For much of the fourth millennium B.C. Palestine supported a number of regional cultures not yet fully differentiated, though none of them apparently has a direct relationship with the preceding Neolithic ones. It is customary to regard the first use of copper for tools and weapons as a major change in the archaeological record (CHALCOLITHIC PERIOD). Its social and economic effects were, however, gradual. It is not the new tools themselves, which long remained secondary to stone ones, but the establishment of settlements in mining and smelting centres, the appearance of specialists in metalworking and the diffusion of their wares through trade which stimulated fresh cultural developments. In Palestine these early metal working communities first appeared in marginal regions: the Dead Sea shores, the northern Negev and the coastal plains, in the earlier fourth millennium B.C. They are best known from a village at Teleilat Ghassul just north of the Dead Sea and on a group of sites in the Beersheba region (Abu Matar, etc.). These people were certainly intrusive, but the location of their original home is uncertain; they almost certainly infiltrated into Palestine from the north, in some cases passing down the coast, in others down the Jordan valley. The picture is somewhat confused by the slightly later penetration of further groups of people from the north at present described by some scholars as the PROTO-URBAN Groups A, B and C.

Hunting is no longer of such importance; agriculture and cattle-breeding provide the food supply. Specialist handicrafts have developed considerably; it is possible that individual villages specialized either in potting, weaving, basket-making, the manufacture of vessels and figurines in stone, bone, ivory or metal. At Ghassul well-built rectangular houses were in some cases decorated with wall-paintings. At Abu Matar large underground dwellings connected by tunnels were used first and only gradually superseded by free-standing houses. A remarkable hoard of copper ritual objects, made c. 3200 B.C., found in a cave at Nahal Mishmar reveals the range and technical skill of contemporary metalsmiths.

A very significant change is marked by the first appearance of towns with closely built houses within enclosure walls, as at Jericho, Tell el Far'ah (North) and Arad, or settlements on sites specially selected for their natural defences as at 'Ai and Ophel in Jerusalem, in the very early third millennium B.C. (EARLY BRONZE AGE). Moving peacefully into the country from the north new settlers brought a distinctive architectural tradition, in which mud brick was extensively used. Flint techniques were further improved and one particularly fine range of pottery, the so-called 'Khirbet Kerak ware', was developed under strong northern influence, c. 2500 B.C. Temples of this period are known

Plate 3 Early Bronze Age pottery, including a bowl of 'Khirbet Kerak ware', from Jericho

at Jericho, Arad and En-Gedi, but the best preserved and equipped sanctuary is one at 'Ai, which to some extent foreshadows the arrangements and furnishings of later Canaanite temples. The first known example of a 'high-place' (*bamah*) was found in the Early Bronze Age levels at Megiddo, with numerous animal bones and broken vases from sacrifices and offerings lying around it. A remarkable series of tombs and charnel houses spanning the whole period have been found near a large fortified site at Bab edh-Dhra' close to the eastern shore of the Dead Sea, facing the Lisan.

The well defended towns of the Early Bronze Age suggest the existence of independent, land-owning city states under established rulers, wary of each other, of nomads from the desert fringes and, at least in the south, perhaps also of the armies of Egypt. Although relations with Mesopotamia were rare throughout the period, contacts with Egypt were much stronger, particularly early in the period.

In the last quarter of the third millennium B.C., after centuries of settled life the *tells* show a marked break in occupation, often accompanied by signs of fire and destruction, followed by a temporary absence of walled settlements and well-built houses.

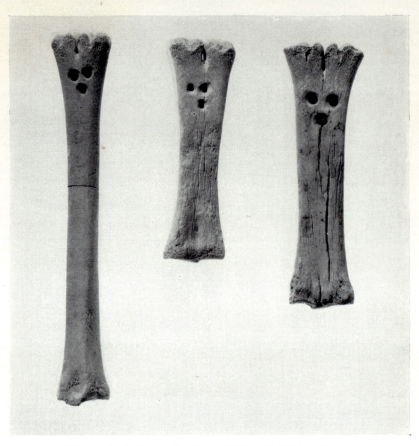

Plate 4   Early Bronze Age bone 'idols' or 'dolls' from Jericho

This can only indicate a break in urban civilization and the intrusion of nomadic peoples. There is also a new repertory of pottery and marked changes in burial customs. Archaeologists vary in their designation of this period; the term *Early to Middle Bronze Age* is used here to denote its essentially transitional character.

This upheaval in Palestine is the local aspect of widespread pressure from the desert fringes into the centres of urban civilization at this time. In Palestine, as in Mesopotamia where texts name them, the main intruders were probably Amorites (*Amurru*).

In Egypt infiltrating Asiatics profited from internal political instability to establish themselves in Sinai and the Delta during the
First Intermediate Period, *c.* 2200–2000 B.C. The whole process
of penetration may have been facilitated by a vigorous donkey
caravan trade through a series of walled settlements in Transjordan, across the Wadi Arabah and through the Negev to the
borders of Egypt.

HISTORIC PALESTINE: THE CANAANITE
CIVILIZATION
c. 1900–1200 B.C.

Urban life returned to Palestine after *c.* 1900 B.C. through
settlers from Syria and Mesopotamia, of Amorite extraction, who
inaugurated the civilization which was to last the best part of
a thousand years and may most conveniently be described as
Canaanite. This word does not appear in historical inscriptions
before the fifteenth century B.C., and even then only in a restricted
sense. But, since it is used in the Old Testament to describe the
major element in the population of Palestine at the entry of the
Israelites in the later thirteenth century B.C., it is the best available
generic term for the culture of Palestine in the second millennium
B.C. Philologically it is used as a term to describe one branch of the
North-Semitic group of languages, including both Hebrew and
Phoenician, the other branch being Aramaic.

Although there are still no local written records the MIDDLE
BRONZE AGE, *c.* 1900–1550 B.C., is the first truly historic period
in Palestine. Now for the first time the records of Egypt, Mesopotamia and Syria throw real light on the structure, and even some
of the personalities, of the urban and pastoral societies of the time.
In the economic, social and linguistic facts they preserve we can
recognize the historical setting—though not the exact date—of the
Hebrew Patriarchs, and the origins of many biblical institutions
(see pp. 36 ff.).

In the eighteenth and seventeenth centuries B.C. Palestine
enjoyed a period of considerable prosperity and influence, though

29

Plate 5   Middle Bronze Age bone inlays from a wooden box, Jericho

the archaeological evidence is still meagre and has to be supplemented by finds from richer sites like Alalakh (Tell 'Atshana) and Ugarit (Ras Shamra) in Syria. Palestine was again a land of independent or loosely confederated city-states, some protected with massive earth ramparts revetted with plastered slopes or cyclopean masonry skirtings. Walls and gateways, temples, administrative buildings, patrician and common houses, shops and warehouses, at sites like Tell Beit Mirsim, Duweir, Hazor, Jericho, Megiddo, Shechem and Nahariyeh illustrate all aspects of urban architecture and city life. A remarkable series of sealed tombs at Jericho contained a wide range of pottery and, most exceptionally of all, textiles, wooden furniture and utensils, basketry and food. Bronze was increasingly used in place of copper for tools and weapons. Egyptian influence is conspicuous in various minor arts—notably furniture, alabaster vessels, and faience figurines, amulets and scarabs. Cretan influence may perhaps be detected in the decoration of ivory inlays.

During the XIIth Dynasty (c. 1991–1786 B.C.) Egypt's strong commercial interest in Palestine was reinforced by growing diplomatic activity in the area, but probably not by any sustained attempt at political domination. To this period belongs one of the most famous of Egyptian stories—the Autobiography of Sinuhe— with a central narrative, based on fact, which relates in some detail the exile of an Egyptian official in Palestine during the reign of Sesostris I (c. 1971–1928 B.C.). In the unsettled period after the end of this dynasty in Egypt Asiatics who had been infiltrating into the Delta from Palestine slowly established a political supremacy during the seventeenth century B.C. (XVth Dynasty), exercising tutelage over most of Egypt. The leaders of these people were known to the Egyptians as *Hikau-khoswet* (Hyksos): 'Princes of Foreign Countries'. In a manner not yet clearly determined much Hyksos power was drawn from the city-states of Palestine; but *Hyksos* may not properly be used as an ethnic or cultural term. Certain artefacts once associated with their name: glacis fortifications, pottery with punctured designs on a black or brown fabric ('Tell el Yahudiyeh Ware') and certain types of scarab, are now seen to be products of the much wider Canaanite civilization.

31

Plate 6   Middle Bronze Age wooden dish and comb, Jericho

Archaeology and 'Genesis'

Into this complex pattern of migrating peoples and reviving urban life in Palestine in the earlier second millennium B.C. events described in Genesis may now be fitted. The geographical background of the first eleven chapters is Mesopotamian rather than

Plate 7   Part of an Egyptian scribe's copy of the 'Autobiography of Sinuhe'

Plate 8   Three 'Tell el-Yahudiyeh' juglets from the name site in Egypt

Palestinian. With the appearance of Abraham in chapter 12 a
narrative with clear historical basis definitely identifies two of the
places whence the Patriarchs had come as Ur in Iraq and Harran
in Syria. As these nomadic tribes moved north, then west, they
took with them the cultural heritage of their homeland. The
legends which inspired the later writers of the early chapters of
Genesis are now known to us in the original form written in
cuneiform script in the Akkadian and Sumerian languages on clay
tablets from Iraq. These tell of antediluvian kings or heroes, of a
Golden Age and of a Flood in many ways similar, if distinct in
theological interpretation, to those related by the later Hebrew
writers. Mesopotamia too was the home of the ziggurat ('Tower
of Babel').

34

Plate 9   The 'Weld-Blundell' prism inscribed with the Sumerian
King Lists from Larsa, Iraq

Cuneiform tablets, particularly those of the eighteenth century B.C. from Mari in Syria, and magical texts used in ceremonies to curse the Pharaoh's enemies from Thebes, Sakkara and Mirgissa in Egypt ('Execration texts' of the XIIth to XIIIth Dynasties) show that the names of people and places associated with the Patriarchs were widely current at this time. Of particular interest are references in the Mari texts to a troublesome bedouin tribe known as the 'Beni-Yamina'. The name is the same as the Old Testament 'Benjaminites' and there may well be some direct connection. Tablets from Nuzi in Iraq, where the population was predominantly Hurrian-speaking, explain much that is obscure in the Old Testament account of the customs observed by the Patriarchs in marriage, adoption, inheritance and land holding. The nearest parallels to the Pentateuchal Law Code are also to be found in Mesopotamian sources, notably the renowned Code of Hammurabi and its precursors. Such was the world in which the Patriarchs moved; still, however, the exact place of the wandering Hebrews is provokingly elusive.

Few problems in Biblical studies have exercised scholars so much as the relation between the Hebrews of Genesis and the *Habiru/Hapiru* mentioned in all important archives of cuneiform tablets throughout the Near East in the second millennium B.C. They occur first in Mesopotamia, *c.* 2000 B.C., then later in texts from Nuzi in Iraq, Mari and Alalakh in Syria, Alishar and Boghazköy in Turkey and Tell el Amarna in Egypt; at Ras Shamra in Syria they were known as the *'prm*. The matter is greatly complicated by the fact that in some cases the *Habiru* seem to be a social class, at others an ethnic group. Whenever they appear they are generally foreigners. They are either household servants, mercenaries or marauding freebooters; very rarely settled communities. In the Old Testament 'Hebrew' is primarily a term used by foreigners or by Hebrews when speaking of themselves to foreigners. It is probable that the Hebrews were part of the group of people known elsewhere as *Habiru*, but not necessarily identical with a specific group referred to in any Near Eastern text.

Although the Biblical account of Joseph's career in Egypt contains much in the way of names and titles, events and stories, which may be closely paralleled in Egyptian texts of the second

Plate 10   Fragmentary tablet inscribed with part of the
Babylonian Creation epic from Kish in Iraq

millennium B.C., there is nothing which can be used to date his life exactly. It was not particularly uncommon for foreigners to rise high in Pharaoh's service during the New Kingdom and Asiatics were normally allowed to graze their cattle in the Delta, as were Jacob's family. It is most probable, however, that Joseph lived during the period of Hyksos rule in Egypt when, as the Biblical account requires, the capital was in the Delta, and easy of access to the Land of Goshen, not, as later, away to the south in Thebes.

The High Tide of Canaanite Culture

The LATE BRONZE AGE denotes a period of about four centuries beginning with the expulsion of the Hyksos rulers from Egypt in the earlier sixteenth century B.C. and ending in the earlier twelfth century with a catastrophic disruption of settled urban life by migrant or dissident peoples, amongst whom Israelites, Aramaeans and 'Sea Peoples' (including Philistines) form distinguishable elements.

Evidence for the earliest phase is scanty, but suggests a swift re-establishment of Egyptian authority following the expulsion of the Hyksos rulers and some violent dislocation of urban life. Of the subsequent resettlement a fine bichrome painted pottery is the most distinctive product. The distribution of this ware, from Tell 'Ajjul to Ras Shamra, and overseas to Cyprus, and conversely the spread of imported Cypriot and Mycenaean wares, from the Aegean, reveals an opening up of Mediterranean and continental trade and communications accompanying the establishment of strong and politically active kingdoms in Egypt (XVIIIth Dynasty), Turkey (Hittites) and north-east Syria (Mitanni).

In the south and on the coastal plain Egypt retained a general control over the principal cities of Canaan. Egyptian stelae and statues were set up in towns and fortresses, particularly those which served or guarded the coastal and inland highways along which Egyptian diplomats and armies travelled to contend with the Hittites and Mitanni for supremacy in Palestine and Syria. In the early fifteenth century B.C. a military aristocracy of Hurrians and Indo-Aryans seized power in some of the principal cities of Palestine, introducing new military equipment like the light war-

Plate 11   Late Bronze Age pendants and ear-rings from Tell el 'Ajjul
in Israel

chariot, scale-armour and the composite bow. They were rapidly
assimilated and left no permanent mark on Canaanite civilization.

Monuments excavated at Ras Shamra and Byblos and some fine
work in ivory and gold from Tell 'Ajjul, Duweir and Megiddo
have revealed the eclectic character of Canaanite art in which
many Egyptian motifs were blended with more local traditions.

The pre-eminent contribution of the Canaanites to the civilized
world was the development of alphabetic writing. While the Near
East at large conducted its commercial, administrative and diplomatic affairs in the Akkadian language and the cuneiform script,

39

(a)

(b)

Plate 12   (a) Glass 'Astarte' figurine from Tell ed-Duweir in Israel, *c.* 1400–1350 B.C.
(b) Baked Clay 'Astarte' plaque from Gezer in Israel, *c.* 1300–1200 B.C.
(c) Faience face for inlay into a statuette from Gezer in Israel, *c.* 1300 B.C.
(d) Late Bronze Age bronze statuette of a deity from Sidon, Lebanon, *c.* 1400–1200 B.C.

(c)

(d)

through professional scribes, in north and south Canaan unknown
scribes were evolving the principle of an alphabet, the first step
to general literacy. The texts from Ras Shamra (Ugarit) in a
cuneiform script, and graffiti from Sinai, Lachish and Gezer with
quasi-pictographic linear signs show diverse approaches by
Canaanites to the same invention.

Canaanite Cults

Although temples, temple furnishings and cult images have

41

been found in a number of places, they would have remained dumb without the texts found at Ras Shamra to speak for them and reveal to us something of the mythology and cults which inspired their creation. The cults of the Canaanites were heavily abused by the writers of the Old Testament and it is only now that we may begin to appreciate their importance for a full understanding of the religious ideas and cult practices of the Old Testament itself. These texts do not offer a comprehensive survey of Canaanite religious beliefs, but they give vivid glimpses of the main deities and the more important festivals, rites and sacrifices at one important capital city.

The only guide we have to the character of these Canaanite deities, since monumental sculpture is rare in Palestine, are various small-scale figures in copper and bronze, sometimes overlaid with gold or silver. Many are extremely crude and were no doubt mass-produced in moulds as votive offerings. Others, which show the deity enthroned or brandishing weapons, may be miniature copies of the cult statues. Commonest of all are baked clay plaques and figurines of nude women carrying various floral and animal attributes. Though generally known as Astarte the lady's identity, even her divinity, is open to question. Whoever she was, if indeed it is always one and the same person represented, these plaques, and various gold pendants associated with her, were presumably fertility charms.

In the late thirteenth and early twelfth centuries B.C. the Israelite invasions and the inroads of the 'Peoples of the Sea' destroyed the political authority of the Canaanites in Palestine. But much of their culture survived in the north among the Phoenician cities of the Lebanon. Thus it was that the Canaanites influenced the Israelites not only during the Conquest, but subsequently through the close diplomatic and commercial contacts which existed between Phoenicia and the southern kingdoms in the earlier first millennium B.C.

EXODUS AND CONQUEST

The Old Testament account of Joshua's conquest suggests that in central Palestine, particularly around Shechem, there were already settled a group of 'Hebrews' who had never been in

Plate 13 Fragmentary tablet with a letter from the ruler of
Byblos to the Pharaoh of Egypt, found at Tell el Amarna, Egypt

Egypt nor taken part in the Exodus (Josh. xxiv; see also Gen. xxxiv).
These people had almost certainly established themselves there in
the fourteenth century B.C. Portions of the diplomatic archives of
the Pharaohs Amenophis III and IV (Akhenaten) from Tell el
Amarna in Egypt include correspondence with the local Canaanite
rulers of Palestine in the earlier fourteenth century B.C. These
reveal considerable political instability with recurrent internal
feuding between rulers, exercising their authority under the close

43

supervision of Egyptian officials, and persistent strife with marauding bands of *Habiru* pressing into the hill country. Even at this time the ruler of Shechem was exceptionally outspoken and independent in his relations with his overlords.

It was another branch of these wandering tribes who went into Egypt and were enslaved there. Although there is no evidence outside the Old Testament for the Israelites' forced labour and later exodus, the Biblical story is generally consistent with known historical events. Early in his reign the Pharaoh Ramses II (1304–1237 B.C.) undertook extensive restorations and rebuildings at Pithom and Ramses, where the Israelites served (Exod. i. 11). About 1230 B.C. his successor the Pharaoh Merneptah, set up a stela at Thebes recording his defeat of the 'people of Israel', who were already in Canaan but not yet settled down. The Exodus may then be broadly dated between *c.* 1280 and 1240 B.C. Archaeological survey has shown that early in the thirteenth century B.C. after a long interval urban life was renewed in Edom, Moab and Ammon. Since these kingdoms feature in the story of the Exodus this provides additional confirmation for dating the episode in the middle of the thirteenth century B.C. and not earlier. A later dating, as will be seen, is also unlikely in terms of the existing historical and archaeological evidence.

Regrettably the most distinctive trait of the Israelites—their religion—is, archaeologically, invisible. So far it has proved impossible to credit them with any distinctive artefact through which their conquest of Palestine might be charted. Destruction levels of the late thirteenth century have been found in a number of *tells* recorded in the Biblical account of Joshua's conquest: notably at Duweir (Lachish), Bethel, Tell el-Hesy (Eglon), Tell Beit Mirsim (Debir) and Hazor—but they might equally well in some, if not in all, cases be the work of Merneptah's armies. In the destruction level at Duweir, for instance, there was a broken bowl with its surface used by an Egyptian tax collector to record wheat deliveries from local harvests in the fourth year of an un-named Pharaoh. Epigraphically this is most likely to be Merneptah and provides a valuable *terminus post quem* for the destruction. Of Joshua's most spectacular triumph—the capture of Jericho—archaeology has failed so far to yield any evidence. In the southern part of Galilee new settlers may be traced penetrating

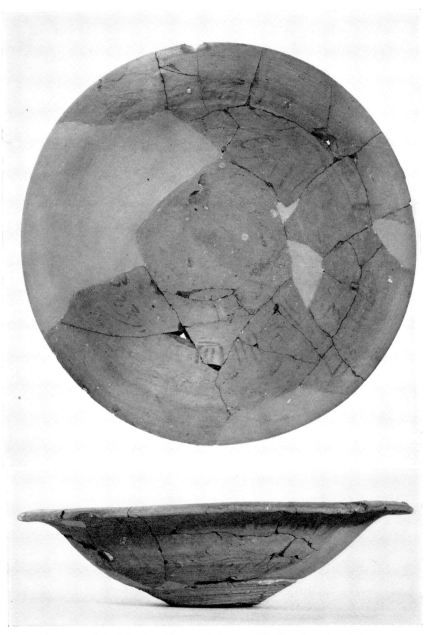

Plate 14   Baked clay bowl (restored) inscribed in Egyptian hieratic from
Tell ed-Duweir in Israel

45

Plate 15   Baked clay anthropoid coffin from Tell el-Yahudiyeh in Egypt,
c. 1220–1150 B.C.

into previously unoccupied regions and finds from Deir 'Alla, a
sanctuary site in Transjordan, reveal nomadic activity at this time,
but in both cases the actors remain anonymous. It is possible that
tablets in an unknown script found at Deir 'Alla hold the clue.

46

Whilst the Israelites were penetrating into Palestine from the east, the impact of the so-called 'Peoples of the Sea' was first felt in the west. They appeared in Palestine in the closing years of the thirteenth century B.C. as mercenaries in the Egyptian service. Virtually identical weapons, distinctive baked clay anthropoid coffins and other artefacts from Beth Shemesh, Beth Shan and Tell el-Far'ah (South) in Palestine, Tell Nabesha and Tell el-Yahudiyeh in the Egyptian Delta and Aniba in Nubia reveal the wide distribution of these troops. Fortresses of this period have been excavated at Ashdod and Gaza.

About 1190 B.C. a large-scale land and sea invasion of Egypt by the 'Peoples of the Sea', including the Philistines, was repulsed by Ramses III, but much of the coastal plain of Palestine from south of Gaza to south of Joppa was settled by Philistines, initially as Egyptian vassals. In this area is concentrated a distinctive type of painted pottery with a slip in different shades of white and decorated with one or two colour designs, which is certainly of Philistine manufacture. Both shapes and designs reflect the cultural influences under which the Philistines passed during the long journey from their original home, probably in the Aegean or West Turkey. The closest parallels have been found at Enkomi in Cyprus. This ware was not made after the later eleventh century B.C., though imitations are current later. The first regular use of iron for tools and weapons was introduced into Palestine by the Philistines who, according to the Old Testament, exercised control over its production.

ISRAEL AND JUDAH: INDEPENDENCE AND VASSALAGE

The rise and brief duration of Judaean and Israelite kingdoms, the maritime and commercial enterprise of the Phoenicians and the westward expansion of the Assyrian Empire are the outstanding episodes in the EARLY IRON AGE between the collapse of the Canaanite political supremacy in Palestine in the twelfth century and the Babylonian captivity of the sixth century B.C.

The period of the Israelite Judges (*c.* 1200–1020 B.C.) is an

47

Plate 16   Baked clay stirrup-jar (restored) in the Philistine style
from Tell el-Far'ah (South) in Israel, c. 1200–1150 B.C.

archaeological Dark Age with scant traces of architectural remains
or artefacts. During this time Philistine power reached its zenith
with the fall of Shiloh, and destruction levels on the *tells* at Tell
Beit Mirsim, Beth-zur, Bethel, Beth Shemesh and Megiddo
probably mark Philistine assaults about 1050 B.C. The reigns of
Saul and David (c. 1020–960 B.C.) are scarcely better represented.
Both men were too heavily engaged in military operations and
political organization to undertake extensive building programmes
and what they did build was largely obliterated by the more
extensive activities of Solomon.

The influence of Phoenicia
Although archaeology still offers a pale reflection of Solomon's legendary glory, largely because his palace and the Temple in Jerusalem are irretrievably lost beneath Herod's Temple platform, the detailed Biblical account of his activities as a builder and merchant-prince may be supplemented from a variety of archaeological sources. Survey and excavation on sites in the Wadi Arabah have revealed extensive exploitation of the local metal ores and the development of Red Sea trade through a port at Ezion-Geber with its own great smelting refinery. The great store-cities and garrison-cities which Solomon established are listed in 1 Kings ix. 15–18; at Gezer, Hazor and Megiddo excavations have disclosed fortified gateways built by his master masons. At Megiddo extensive installations for stabling horses, though built in the following century, are no doubt modelled on Solomon's original plan. In many of his commercial enterprises Solomon was closely associated with Hiram, King of Tyre, who provided the specialist craftsmen and timber used in building the Temple. This important piece of information, combined with the full, if sometimes obscure, description of the Temple in 1 Kings vi have allowed archaeologists to reconstruct it with reasonable accuracy.

The plan of the Temple was a standard one, as the best parallels—at Tell Tainat in Syria and Tell Arad in Israel—make clear; in both cases these temples, as in Jerusalem, were closely associated with a 'royal' residence. For the Temple's elaborate internal decoration reference must be made to the numerous fragments of carved ivory, many of them furniture inlays, found at Nimrud (biblical Calah) in Iraq, which had reached the great Assyrian palaces and fortresses there as tribute and spoils from Phoenicia and Syria between the ninth and seventh centuries B.C. The freestanding *cherubim* and the wooden panels which lined the walls of the Temple, richly carved with floral patterns and *cherubim*, were but large-scale versions of the varied motifs found in abundance on these ivories. Those made in Phoenicia are distinguished by the prevalence of themes derived from Egyptian art, for commercial links with Egypt were as vigorous in Phoenicia in the tenth century as they had been earlier in the Canaanite period. The various bronze and stone furnishings of the Temple may be illustrated from a number of sites in Palestine and Cyprus, though

D　　　　　49

(a)

not of the fine workmanship or on the scale which undoubtedly distinguished those in the Jerusalem Temple.

The use of ivory, both for the decoration of buildings and furniture, is clearly attested elsewhere in the Old Testament (1 Kings x. 18; xxii. 39; Amos iii. 15; vi. 4). At Samaria remnants were found from the carved ivory decoration of the palace that Ahab, married to the Phoenician princess Jezebel, built there c. 850 B.C.

Plate 17 (a) Ivory plaque carved in the Egyptian manner with a 'sacred tree' and human attendants from Nimrud in Iraq, eighth to seventh century B.C.

(b) Syrian lyre-player carved on an ivory pyxis fragment from Nimrud in Iraq, eighth to seventh century B.C.

(c) Ivory plaque carved with an illegible royal name guarded by sphinxes in the Egyptian manner; Nimrud, Iraq, eighth to seventh century B.C.

(b)   (c)

Plate 18   Iron Age pottery from Jerusalem, *c.* 800 B.C.

It was not only in commerce, art and architecture that Phoenicia exerted a deep influence on Palestine. Phoenician deities—the old Canaanite Pantheon—filtered into Palestine in the train of Phoenician princesses married to Solomon and Ahab (2 Kings xxiii. 13; 1 Kings xviii. 19), as definite royal policy under Manasseh (687/686–642 B.C.) (2 Kings xxi) and as part of a persistent tendency in all classes to worship the forces of nature controlling fertility, climate and prosperity. The Old Testament prophets constantly inveighed against this resurrection of the old pagan deities, but baked clay female figurines and extra-mural shrines on Ophel in Jerusalem indicate the prevalence of unorthodox cults and deep-seated popular superstitions. One type of object closely associated with the rites of these unorthodox cults was the *hamman* (2 Chron. xxxiv. 4; A.V. trans. 'images'), or incense-altar, clearly represented on a much later stone altar from Palmyra in Syria. This was given to the University of Oxford in the middle of the eighteenth century. In part the altar's inscription reads 'in the month of September of the year 396 (85 A.D.), this *hamman* and this altar were made and offered by Lišamš and Zebida. . . .'

52

Plate 19   Stone altar from Palmyra, dated A.D. 85, showing an incense-
altar

The Canaanite script invented during the second millennium B.C. soon developed into two distinct, if very similar, ways of writing the same alphabet: 'Early Hebrew' and 'Phoenician'. The 'Early Hebrew' script had begun to acquire its distinctive character by *c*. 1000 B.C. (in the schoolboy's exercise known as the Gezer Calendar) and was used until the sixth century B.C., whereafter emerged 'Square Hebrew', the parent of the classical Hebrew script. Among the rare monumental inscriptions in this script are two of outstanding historical importance: the 'Mesha Stone' recording the triumph of Mesha, King of Moab (2 Kings iii. 4), over Israel *c*. 840 B.C. and the inscription from Jerusalem recording the completion of Hezekiah's tunnel, *c*. 700 B.C. (2 Kings xx. 20). It is much more commonly found on potsherds noting tax or revenue returns, notably an eighth-century group from Samaria, stone seals belonging to royal officers or private persons, inscribed weights, jar handles with royal seal impressions, *c*. 710– 650 B.C., and as fitters' marks on ivories and stones.

The 'Phoenician' script is of even greater cultural significance since, adopted and adapted by the Greeks, it was to be ancestral to all Western alphabets. Whereas examples of the 'Early Hebrew' script are virtually confined to Palestine, 'Phoenician' inscriptions have been found throughout the Mediterranean world, diffused through their great commercial enterprise.

The Assyrian Menace

A common cultural tradition and mutual interests made the relations between Palestine and Phoenicia advantageous and peaceful; it was to be otherwise with Assyria, as the Old Testament so vividly reveals. The inscriptions and monumental reliefs set up by many Assyrian kings, both at home in their palaces at Nimrud, Nineveh and Khorsabad and abroad in the cities they occupied, illustrate their military activities and offer a valuable complement to the biblical account of their relations with Israel and Judah. Indeed it was an Assyrian relief from Nimrud, showing Jehu, son of Omri, paying tribute to Shalmaneser III (858–824 B.C.) found by A. H. Layard in 1846, which first revealed the great potential of archaeology in biblical studies.

Unlike Egypt and Phoenicia, Assyria exerted little or no cultural

Plate 20 (a) Modern impression of the seal of a certain 'Hosea'
(b) Modern impression of the seal of 'Mikneiah, son of Yehomelek'

Plate 21 Ivory inlay from Nimrud, Iraq, showing the fitter's mark on the back

55

Plate 22   Baked clay handle from a storage jar naming the city of Socoh,
c. 700 B.C.

influence on Palestine during the time of its supremacy. Successive
Assyrian kings during the eighth and seventh centuries B.C.
exploited the division between Judah and Israel to exact tribute
and spoils, to maintain puppet kings and, when necessary, to exert
their authority by force of arms. At Samaria, Tell Beit Mirsim,
Megiddo and Tell en-Nasbeh substantial city walls and gateways
reflect the insecurity of the period. Sennacherib's reliefs in his palace
at Nineveh depicting the siege of Lachish in 701 B.C. bear a very
close resemblance to the structure of the town revealed in level

III at Tell ed-Duweir and give a very detailed picture of the Assyrian assault. At this time, as part of arrangements to meet the threat of Assyrian invasion, Hezekiah reorganized the system of collecting and storing taxes received in kind. They were placed in large jars, which contained a standard official measure and their handles bore the words 'Belonging to the king' above a four-winged beetle with below it the name of one of the four main store-cities: Hebron, Socoh, Ziph and *mmšt* (probably meaning Jerusalem). Some time after *c.* 700 B.C. the beetle was replaced by a double-winged symbol, which probably marks subjection to Assyrian domination.

Babylonian and Persian Overlords

The Babylonian captivity in the early to mid sixth century B.C., the slow repopulation and return to prosperity under the Persian administration from the late fifth to fourth centuries B.C., the growing influence of Hellenism under the Ptolemies and Seleucids, the bitter internal feuds of the Jewish priesthood, and the Roman occupation are the main events of the period between the end of Assyrian domination in the late seventh century B.C. and the crucifixion of Christ in the first century A.D. Now for the first time in Palestine archaeological sources, still very sparse for the first three centuries, are supplementary to the wide range of historical evidence which has survived in Greek, Latin, Hebrew and Aramaic. Increasingly documents written on ostraca and papyrus, inscribed coins and monumental inscriptions reveal significant details of public and private life. During this period the literature of the Old Testament was united more or less in the form we now have it and archaeological excavation has revealed contemporary biblical manuscripts of outstanding significance for understanding the original Hebrew text.

No archaeological finds from Palestine reveal so immediately as the so-called 'Lachish Letters' the threat of foreign conquest to which the country was constantly exposed. These documents, written in ink on potsherds, were found among the debris of the last destruction level in one of the guard rooms built into the city gate at Tell ed-Duweir. Most scholars regard them as part of the correspondence between the local military governor and an officer

57

in an outpost during the anxious months before the city fell to Nebuchadnezzar II and the Babylonian army *c.* 589/588 B.C. The language and style of these letters is that of the Judaeans in the time of Jeremiah, who graphically describes the events of this troubled period (e.g. Jer. xxxiv. 7). At Jerusalem the devastation wrought by Nebuchadnezzar's army in 587 B.C. may be seen on Ophel, where the great stone terraces (? *Millo*), upon which the pre-exilic city was built, collapsed down the slope so that when Nehemiah inspected the walls of Jerusalem more than a century later 'there was no place for the beast that was under me to pass' (Neh. ii. 14). Among clay tablets inscribed in the Akkadian language found in excavations at Babylon are lists of rations issued to prisoners held in the city between 595 and 570 B.C. Listed among them are Jehoiachin, King of Judah, captured in 598 B.C. (2 Kings xxiv), five royal princes and other Judaean captives.

The thoroughness of the Babylonian devastation and subsequent deportations is clearly reflected in the paucity of archaeological evidence for the sixth century B.C. Only when the Persians replaced the Babylonians as overlords and Cyrus allowed the Judaeans to return from their Babylonian exile following an edict of *c.* 538 B.C., quoted in the Old Testament both in its original Aramaic (Ezra vi. 3–5) and local Hebrew form (Ezra i. 2–4), is it possible to trace reviving urban life, but then only in a small area around Jerusalem. It was probably a couple of centuries or more before Palestine was once again as densely populated as it had been in the later seventh century B.C.

Within the administrative system they established (Dan. iii. 2–3, 27; vi. 2–7; Esther iii. 12; Ezra viii. 36) the Persian rulers allowed the people of Palestine considerable independence. The seat of a governor, appointed by the Persians, if not actually a foreigner, was found at Tell ed-Duweir and what may be the tomb of another was excavated at Tell el-Far'ah (South) equipped with a bronze bed and stool, as well as fine silver tableware. These vessels and others from isolated tombs, notably at Gezer, and coin hoards containing jewellery, illustrate the wide currency at this time of fine metal-work made to standard patterns in workshops closely associated with the courts of Persian governors. It was these administrators and the rich mercantile classes who used the great variety of Greek pottery imported into Palestine at this time. Greek in-

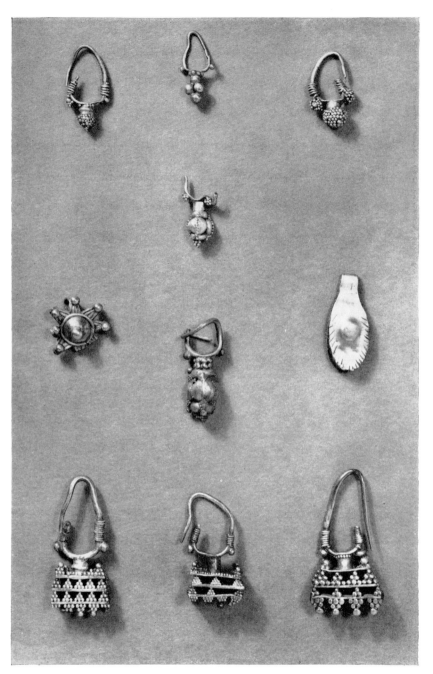

Plate 23   Silver ear-rings and pendants from a coin hoard buried by
c. 450 B.C.

59

Plate 24 Fragment from the side of an Attic red-figure lekythos (small jug) found at Tell el-Farʿah (South) in Israel

fluence was also reflected in the advent of coinage struck in imitation of the Attic drachma with the legend: *YEHUD:* Judah. About this time Arab nomads had overrun most of the Negev and southern Transjordan (Neh. vi. 1, 6) reviving the rich trade in spices and incense from Arabia. The appearance of small limestone incense altars, exactly like those found in south Arabia, some crudely decorated, on sites in southern Palestine reveal the opening up of a route to the Mediterranean coast. In a cave in the Wadi Daliyeh, north of Jericho, papyri and sealings have been found dating *c.* 375–335 B.C. These legal documents, written in Aramaic,

Plate 25   Palestinian lamps from *c.* 2000 B.C. to A.D. 100

were left by a group of refugees, probably from the armies of Alexander the Great in 331 B.C., who all died in the cave.

When, after Alexander's death in 323 B.C., his generals divided his Empire among themselves, Palestine was ruled first by the Ptolemies of Egypt until 198 B.C., then briefly by the Seleucids of Syria until 142 B.C., when the Jews asserted their independence under the Hasmoneans (1 Macc. i-xvi).

PALESTINE IN THE GRAECO-ROMAN WORLD

The profound effect of Hellenistic influence on Palestine is evident even from the most cursory examination of the architecture and artefacts found in buildings of this period at Samaria, Gezer and Beth-zur. The third-century rock-cut tombs at Marisa with their animal paintings, Greek inscriptions and graffiti and the second-century palace of a certain Hyrcanus at Arak al Amir, west of Amman, recorded by Josephus (*Ant.* 12. IV. ii), indicate the range and penetration of western styles in art and architecture. Techniques and styles of potting changed radically to conform with the fashions of great Greek potting centres like Athens and

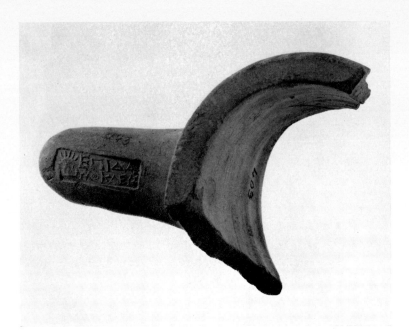

Plate 26 Handle from a Rhodian wine-jar stamped 'Damokles',
c. 220–180 B.C.

Corinth: the fabrics were thinner and fired to higher tempera-
tures; the long-lived Palestinian saucer-lamp was superseded by
the nozzle-lamp of the Greek World. Metal utensils and jewellery
followed western patterns; coins and gems bear Hellenized
devices. Stamped wine jar handles, found in great quantity at sites
like Beth-zur and Samaria, testify to the popularity of wine imported from the Aegean, for each handle bears in Greek the name
of the potter or magistrate of the year.

Since the Hellenistic legacy formed so much of their own
culture the Roman acquisition of Palestine in 63 B.C. did not
greatly affect the course of its cultural development. Indeed it was
largely through the remarkable building activities of Herod the
Great (37–4 B.C.), a man of Edomite origin who ruled as a
Roman vassal, that Hellenism, which he so greatly admired, left
its most enduring mark on the soil of Palestine. Herod's ambiva-
lent attitude is best exemplified by the contrast between the
magnificent pagan temple he built at Samaria-Sebaste in honour

of Caesar Augustus and his complete reconstruction of the Temple in Jerusalem to placate Jewish feeling. Inscriptions in Greek from the Temple have survived, warning Gentiles that they entered the inner courts at peril of their life (Acts xxi. 28). At Samaria, Jerusalem and Caesarea Herod erected great forums, stadiums and theatres, creating cities to the standard Roman pattern. The deep insecurity of his position is, however, tellingly revealed in a whole series of great fortresses, each with a pleasure-palace for himself, in the Judaean wilderness, at sites like Masada, the Herodium and Alexandrium. Herod left Palestine rich and prosperous, but as sorely divided in its political as in its cultural allegiances.

Among Palestine's neighbours the most powerful and influential were the Nabataeans in the east (Mark vi. 17–29; Luke xiii. 32; 2 Cor. xi. 32). Originally of Arabian stock they had established themselves in ancient Edom after the Persian occupation with their capital at Petra, whence they exercised considerable authority from the first century B.C. until the second century A.D. Their wealth and influence depended on control of the caravan trade which passed through Petra to Syria and Palestine, bringing goods from Arabia, India and beyond. Field surveys have shown their mastery in creating an agricultural economy, by skilful conservation of scanty water supplies, in areas apparently bleak and uninhabitable. Cities, villages and fortresses in the Negev of southern Palestine and in Transjordan demonstrate that their architectural and artistic genius was no less impressive. One of their most enduring achievements was a pottery unbelievably thin and fragile, generally bowls, painted with stylized floral and leaf patterns. It is fragments of this pottery which have revealed the extent and intensity of Nabataean settlement.

Such are the more enduring and impressive aspects of the world which the Gospels so vividly describe, moving rapidly from the great cosmopolitan cities like Jerusalem and Caesarea, to smaller ones like Samaria and Jericho, and thence into the country-side where life, save for changing fashions in dress, personal ornaments and daily utensils, varied remarkably little over the centuries. It was amongst the rural community that Christ grew up and spent most of his brief ministry; upon this archaeology can throw no direct light. It has to be content with increasing knowledge of the cities and communities through which he passed,

Plate 27   Nabataean pottery from Petra

and the public figures he encountered. In 1961, for the first time,
a Latin inscription was found, at Caesarea, bearing the name of
Pontius Pilate, procurator of Judea *c.* A.D. 26–36. Far commoner
are stone boxes, in which the bones of the dead were placed after
the flesh had decayed, bearing roughly incised names like Simon,
Martha, Mary, John, Judas, and many others, so familiar to
Christ. History carefully conceals whether any of these ossuaries
was that of one of the simple people who have found immortality
in the Gospels. But such minor discoveries are totally over-
shadowed by finds since 1947 in caves along the western shores
of the Dead Sea. At first accidentally, and then through systematic
search and excavation, they have yielded an immense variety of
manuscripts, revealing very vividly the beliefs and practices of
certain Jewish sects at this time.

Plate 28   Roman pottery and glass of the first century A.D., Jericho

The Dead Sea Scrolls

Eleven caves in the vicinity of the communal centre of a Jewish sect, probably Essene, at Khirbet Qumran near the north-western shore of the Dead Sea have produced remnants of the community's manuscript library. These papyrus and parchment documents were deposited in caves for safety, wrapped in linen and sealed in baked clay jars, early in the First Jewish Revolt against Rome, c. A.D. 66. Most of them date from the third century B.C. to the first century A.D.; the earliest are primarily biblical, the later ones sectarian works for the use of the community. Further south in the Wadi Murabba'at and at Nahal Hever and Nahal Se'elim caves have produced fragmentary Biblical manuscripts of the first and second centuries A.D., legal documents in Hebrew, Aramaic and Greek, letters from Bar Kochba, leader of the Second Jewish Revolt against Rome, c. A.D. 132–5, and the earliest known Hebrew papyrus, of the seventh century B.C. In the course of excavations

E   65

Plate 29   Jar of the type used to store the
'Dead Sea Scrolls'

in the zealot stronghold at Masada, which fell to the Romans in A.D. 73, a number of fragmentary scrolls have been found, notably from the text of Ben Sirah (Ecclesiasticus), in Hebrew, from Psalms, Leviticus and a sectarian text, known previously only from Qumran Cave IV (the so-called Angelic Liturgy).

The importance of these scrolls is manifold. They show what early Hebrew documents and scripts looked like and throw important light on the contemporary spoken language. The early history of Judaism is revealed as far more complex than was previously supposed and the institutions and liturgical practices of the Qumran community may be seen to have remarkable similarities to those of the early Christian Church. Most significant of all, perhaps, the texts of the Old Testament books are about a thousand years older than the oldest previously known Hebrew manuscripts and bring us much closer to the original form in which these books were written down.

The sack of Jerusalem by Titus in A.D. 70 provides an appropriate end to this brief survey. At the fall of the city the Temple was ruthlessly destroyed, never to be rebuilt. When the Emperor Hadrian came to recreate the city it was as a Roman colony, named Aelia Capitolina, in which no Jews might live. The ancient city of Ophel lay outside its walls, a quarry for the new.

Bibliography

The following book-list is restricted to works in English which can be easily obtained through any good public library. Books marked with an asterisk, available in cheap editions, would form the core of a private reference library.

ATLASES

L. H. Grollenberg, *Atlas of the Bible*, trans. and ed. by J. M. H. Reid and H. H. Rowley.

*H. G. May (Ed.), *Oxford Bible Atlas*, Oxford, 1962.

*H. H. Rowley, *The Teach Yourself Bible Atlas*, London, 1960.

GENERAL

Y. Aharoni, *The Land of the Bible*, London, 1967.

*R. D. Barnett, *Illustrations of Old Testament History*, British Museum, 1966.

G. R. Driver, *Semitic Writing: from Pictograph to Alphabet*, Oxford, (rev. ed. 1954).

J. Gray, *The Canaanites*, London, 1964.

D. B. Harden, *The Phoenicians*, London, 1962.

J. B. Pritchard, *The Ancient Near East in Pictures*, Princeton, 1954.

H. H. Rowley, *From Joseph to Joshua*, London, 1950.

Y. Yadin, *The Art of Warfare in Biblical Lands*, London, 1963.

R. de Vaux, *Ancient Israel, its Life and Institutions*, London, 1965.

ARCHAEOLOGY

General:

*W. F. Albright, *The Archaeology of Palestine*, Pelican Books.

*   ,,   *From Stone Age to Christianity*, Doubleday Anchor Book, New York, 1957.

E. Anati, *Palestine Before the Hebrews*, New York, 1963.

*M. Burrows, *What Mean these Stones?*, Meridian Books, London, 1957.

J. Finegan, *Light from the Ancient Past, the Archaeological Background of Judaism and Christianity*, Oxford, 1959.

J. Gray, *Archaeology and the Old Testament World*, London, 1962.

*K. M. Kenyon, *Archaeology in the Holy Land*, London, 1965.
    ,,   *Amorites and Canaanites*, London, 1966.
D. Winton Thomas (Ed.), *Archaeology and Old Testament Study*, Oxford, 1967.
G. E. Wright, *Biblical Archaeology*, London, 1957.

Sites:
*A. S. Kapelrud, *The Ras Shamra Discoveries and the Old Testament*, Basil Blackwell, Oxford, 1965.
*K. M. Kenyon, *Digging up Jericho*, London, 1965.
    ,,   *Jerusalem, excavating* 3000 *years of history*, London, 1967.
*J. T. Milik, *Ten Years of Discovery in the Wilderness of Judea*, S.C.M. Press, 1959.
J. B. Pritchard, *Gibeon, where the sun stood still*, Princeton, 1962.
G. E. Wright, *Shechem, the biography of a Biblical City*, London, 1965.
Y. Yadin, *Masada, Herod's Fortress and the Zealots' last stand*, London, 1966.

TEXTS
J. B. Pritchard, *Ancient Near Eastern Texts relating to the Old Testament*, Princeton, 1955.
D. Winton Thomas (Ed.), *Documents from Old Testament Times*, London, 1958.
*G. Vermes, *The Dead Sea Scrolls in English*, Pelican Books, 1962.
*G. E. Wright and R. Fuller, *The Book of the Acts of God, Modern Christian Scholarship interprets the Bible*, Pelican Books, 1965.

The results of current research in Palestine and adjoining countries are published regularly in the PALESTINE EXPLORATION QUARTERLY, the journal of the Palestine Exploration Fund, and in LEVANT, the journal of the British School of Archaeology in Jerusalem. Membership of the Fund and the School entitles the subscriber to copies of these journals and the use of the Fund's library in London, among other benefits. Details of membership can be obtained by writing to the Secretary, Palestine Exploration Fund, 2 Hinde Mews, Marylebone Lane, London, W.1.

EGYPT		PALESTINE		MESOPOTAMIA
	A.D.		A.D.	
Roman Empire		Roman Empire		Parthians
	B.C.		B.C.	
	30			
			140	
Ptolemaic Dynasty		Seleucid and Ptolemaic Dynasties		Seleucid Dynasty
	330		330	
Achaemenid Empire		Achaemenid Empire		Achaemenid Empire
	500		500	
		Babylonian Captivity Divided Monarchy		Neo-Babylonian Period
				Neo-Assyrian Period
The Late Period		United Monarchy		
	1000		1000	Middle Babylonian and Middle Assyrian Periods
The New Kingdom		Joshua and Judges The Late Bronze Age		The Kassite Period
	1500		1500	
The IInd. Intermediate Period		The Middle Bronze Age		The Old Babylonian Period
The Middle Kingdom				The Isin-Larsa Period
	2000		2000	
The Ist. Intermediate Period		The Early to Middle Bronze Period		The Ur III Period The Akkadian Period
The Old Kingdom		The Early Bronze Age		The Early Dynastic Period
Proto-Dynastic Period	3000		3000	
		The Proto-Urban Period		The Jamdat Nasr Period
		The Chalcolithic Period		The Uruk Period
Pre-Dynastic Period	4000		4000	The 'Ubaid Period
				South *North*
		The Pottery Neolithic Period		Halaf
	5000		5000	Eridu Samarra Hassuna
	6000		6000	Jarmo
		The Pre-Pottery Neolithic Period		
	7000		7000	

Diagrammatic Chronological Chart

71